Zoom Video Conferencing Tutorial

Stephen P. Tubbs, P.E.
formerly of the
Pennsylvania State University,
currently an
industrial consultant

1344 Firwood Dr.
Pittsburgh, PA 15243

NOTICE TO THE READER

The author does not warrant or guarantee any of the products, equipment or software described herein or accept liability for any damages resulting from their use.

Zoom is a trademark owned by Zoom Video Communications, Inc.

Microsoft Teams is a trademark owned by Microsoft Corporation

Cisco WebEx is a trademark owned by Cisco Systems, Inc.

Facebook is a trademark owned by Facebook, Inc.

Google is a trademark owned by Google LLC.

ISBN 978-0-9819753-7-5

CONTENTS

INTRODUCTION

More than ever before computers and the internet allow video conferencing.

Now using computer video conferencing software like Zoom, people can see others on a computer screen as they speak and listen to them. Large numbers of people, sometimes in meetings up to 10,000, can view a live presenter without traveling to a meeting site. In smaller meetings up to 1,000 participants can see and communicate with each other over their computers.

Video conferencing by computer is now being done with Boy Scout meetings, business meetings, friends' gab sessions, college courses and many other groups.

Many college and high school courses are given online. These online courses have students and prerecorded instructor's presentations or live instructor presentations. With video conferencing the students can ask the instructor questions during the presentation.

In 2020 the COVID-19 virus suddenly created a large demand for video conferencing. Many office workers began to work from home using their computers to video conference with other workers and customers. Many university and school classes began to be video-conferenced.

The main objective of this book is to teach the beginner how to use the BASIC version of Zoom's video conferencing software. The BASIC version of Zoom is free to individuals. It is designed for both those attending or hosting video conferences. Zoom has many built-in options. The goal of this book is for the reader to be able to comfortably attend or host a simple meeting with Zoom.

A secondary objective of this book is to provide some information on other video conferencing software. Some of these software programs have free toned-down working versions.

The author makes no conclusion that one software is better than another. The reader should contact the companies and determine for himself which product is best for his needs.

The author of this book has observed rapid modifications of the video conferencing software as the COVID-19 virus forced large numbers of people to switch from live meetings to video conferenced meetings. As the numbers of users increased, the video conferencing software companies rapidly improved their products. The improvements are good, but it also meant that video conferencing users may see slightly different software than described in this book. Current software details may not be exactly the same as described here.

Throughout this book the reader will note words printed in italics. Italics are used whenever they are a direct copy of commands or labels used in the Zoom video conferencing software. For example, Zoom has the executable statement "Sign In". When this is referred to in the text of this book it is printed as *Sign In*.

Stephen Tubbs

1.0 VIDEO CONFERENCING BASICS

A conference is a formal interchange of views in a meeting of two or more people. A video conference is a conference with participants in different locations linked by audio and video devices.

In traditional conferences the speaker speaks directly to the listeners, usually in the same room. Being in the same room, the speaker can see the reaction of his words on the faces of the listeners. Without a spoken word from a listener, but by reading listener's body language, the speaker can repeat or clarify points that may have confused some of the listeners. The speaker can also more easily see the urgency expressed by some of the listeners. That could also cause him to clarify what he had said. These things are more difficult when video conferencing. The speaker is limited in the number of faces he can see at one time and clues, like listeners talking with each other, may be missed.

The adept video conference presenter adapts his presentations to the video conferencing system and learns to read clues from his listeners.

For the listeners, video conferencing may not be too different from in person conferencing.

2.0 ZOOM

The Zoom video conferencing software is used to make presentations from a single personal computer, Mac, Android or iPhone through the internet to audiences of one to thousands of attendees. It is used by both lay people and professionals.

Zoom was founded in 2011. It is made by Zoom Video Communications, Inc. and was valued at $16 billion when it went public in 2019. More information about Zoom can be found by going through the internet at https://zoom.us/ or phoning (888) 799-9666.

2.1 SALES INFORMATION FROM A ZOOM WEBSITE

The below was found on https://zoom.us/about/.

"Our mission
To make video communication frictionless

Our vision
Video communication empowering people to accomplish more

Our values
We care for our company, customers, community, teammates, and ourselves

Our culture
Delivering happiness

Zoom helps businesses and organizations bring their teams together in a frictionless environment to get more done. Our easy, reliable cloud platform for video, voice, content sharing, and chat runs across mobile devices, desktops, telephones, and room systems. Zoom is publicly traded on Nasdaq (ZM) and headquartered in San Jose, California."

2.2 ZOOM COMPUTER SYSTEM REQUIREMENTS

To use Zoom video conferencing software a user should have a computer with a speaker and microphone. It is possible to use Zoom without a webcam camera although it is much better to have one. Practically all computers come with a built in speaker. Now many laptops are also made with a built-in webcam camera and microphone. Zoom operates on various Windows and Mac systems. Check for compatibility on: https://support.zoom.us/hc/en-us/articles/201362023-System-Requirements-for-PC-Mac-and-Linux.

The following applies to Zoom Version5.0.4.

Supported Operating Systems

macOS X with macOS 10.7 or later
Windows 10 (note: Enterprise. S Mode is not supported)
Windows 8 or 8.1
Windows 7
Windows Vista with SP1 or later
Windows XP with SP3 or later
Ubuntu 12.04 or higher
Mint 17.1 or higher
Red Hat Enterprise Linux 6.4 or higher
Oracle Linux 6.4 or higher
CentOS 6.4 or higher
Fedora 21 or higher
OpenSUSE 13.2 or higher
ArchLinux (64-bit only)

System Requirements

An internet connection – broadband wired or wireless (3G or 4G/LTE)
Speakers and a microphone – built-in or USB plug-in or wireless Bluetooth
A webcam or HD webcam - built-in or USB plug-in or a HD cam or HD camcorder with video capture card

Processor and RAM Requirements

Minimum single core 1 GHz processor
Recommended dual core or higher (i3/i5/i7 or AMD equivalent) 4 GBb

Supported Tablet and Mobile Devices

Surface PRO 2 or higher running Win 8.1 or higher
iOS and Android devices
Blackberry devices

2.3 ZOOM PARTICIPANTS AND HOSTS

Each Zoom meeting has a host and one or more participants.

The host sets up and generally controls the meeting. He should have a good understanding of Zoom video conferencing software. A host is similar to a professor in a classroom or a moderator at a speaking event. The host should have some Zoom practice before running an important Zoom meeting.

The participants do not need to understand Zoom video conferencing software as well as the host. They can speak to the host and other participants, but only with the permission of the host. The participant's controls are relatively easy to use. A participant can be very effective in a meeting the first time he uses Zoom.

2.4 ZOOM ON A PC

2.4.1 FREE BASIC VERSION OF ZOOM

The free BASIC version of Zoom only has two major limitations. It will not allow meetings of three or more people to be longer than 40 minutes and will not allow more than 100 people in a meeting. Versions of Zoom that are not free have more capabilities, but for the beginner, they are usually not needed.

The webpage at https://zoom.us/pricing lists the different versions of Zoom including the free BASIC version. A partial description of the BASIC version features is in Figure 1.

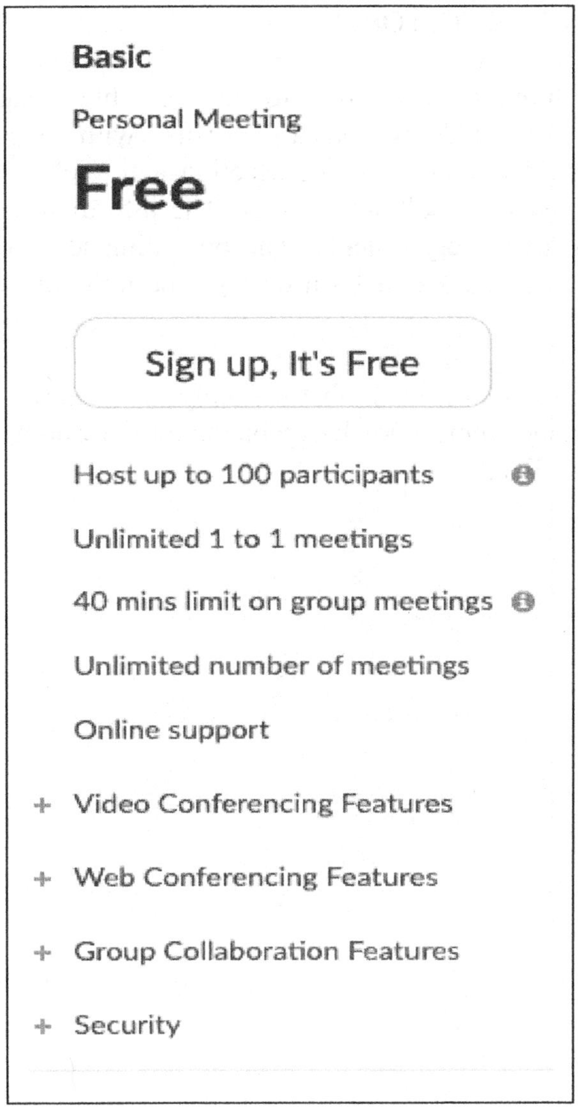

Figure 1 Brief description of the free Zoom BASIC video conferencing software. From https://zoom.us/pricing.

2.4.2 ZOOM'S OWN TRAINING AND TUTORIALS

Zoom's free online training can be found on https://support.zoom.us/hc/en-us/sections/201740096-Training. That address leads to websites with Live Training Webinars, Zoom Video Tutorials, Recorded Training Sessions, Meeting and Webinar Best Practices and Resources, and Zoom Online Events Consulting Services. The information in these websites is helpful. However, instruction is given very quickly. The beginning learner, if he doesn't have instant perfect recall, will have to go back and forth through the training videos and take many notes to learn from them.

The training offered in this book differs in that it simply shows how to participate and host a simple meeting. As a user becomes more knowledgeable about the Zoom program the training offered by Zoom will be more beneficial.

2.4.3 INSTALLING ZOOM BASIC DIRECTLY

To install and start the free BASIC version of Zoom on a PC:

1) Go to https://zoom.us/pricing. Figure 2 appears

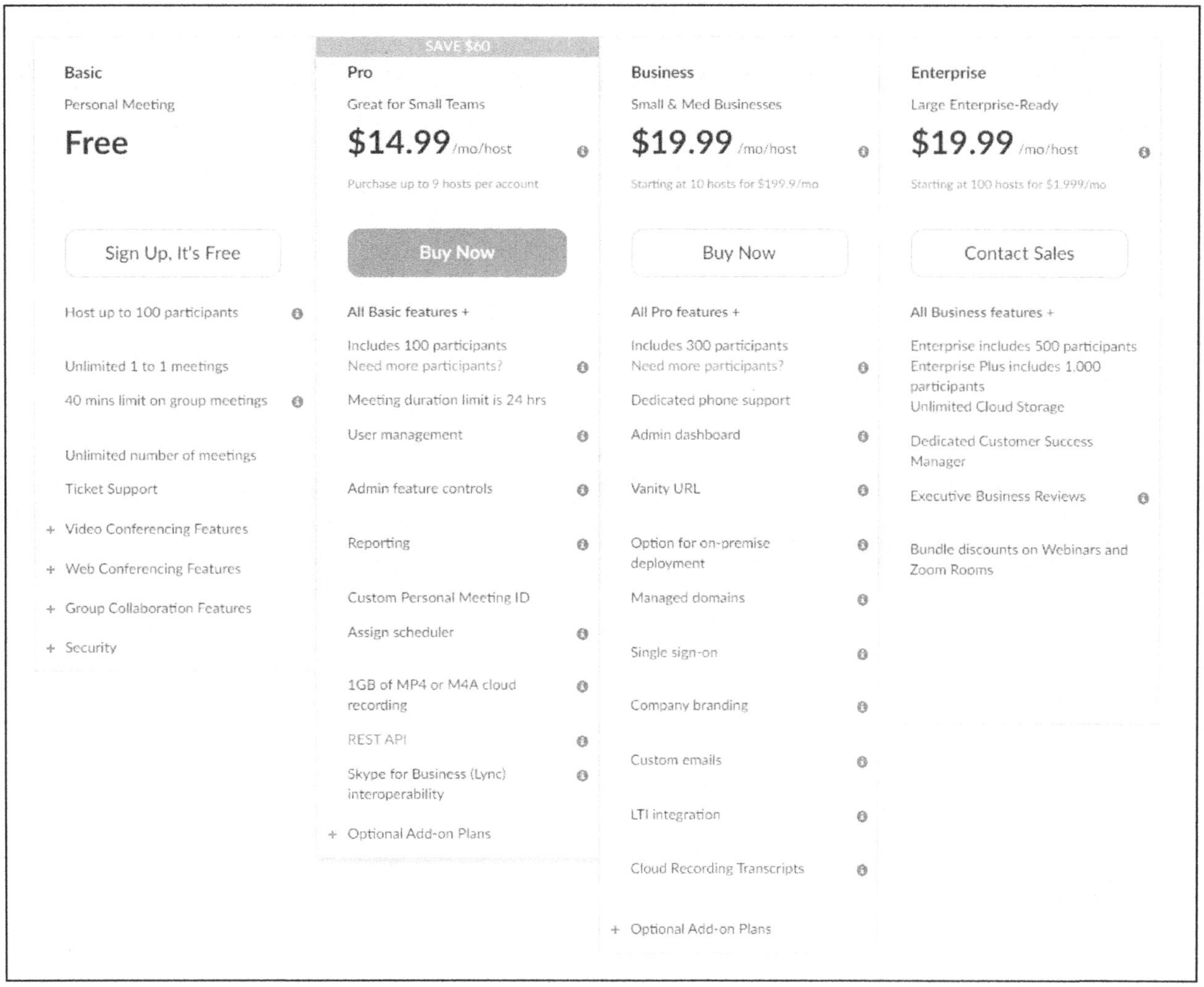

Figure 2 Zoom Meeting Plans. From https://zoom.us/pricing.

2) In the BASIC window left-click on *Sign up, It's Free*. Figure 3 appears. Notice that the text in Figure 3 and many of the following Figures is light and tiny. Making the text darker and larger in these figures would have substantially increased the size and cost of the book. If possible the student should be working with a computer and an actual copy of Zoom as he goes through this book.

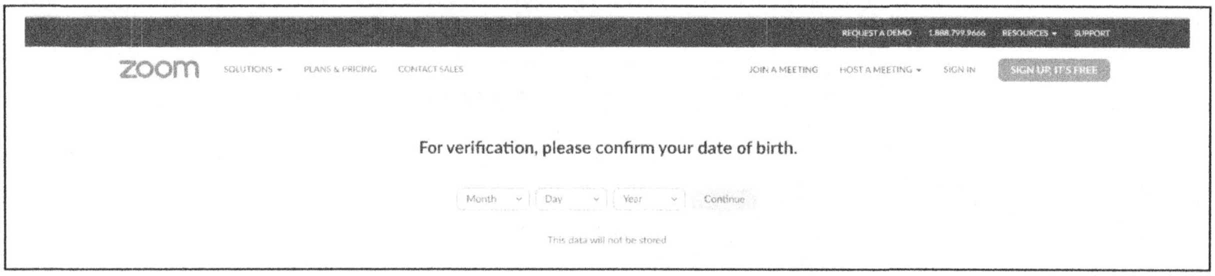

Figure 3 Zoom Verification webpage.

3) Confirm your date of birth and left-click on *Continue*.
4) In the BASIC window left-click on *Sign up, It's Free*. Figure 4 appears.

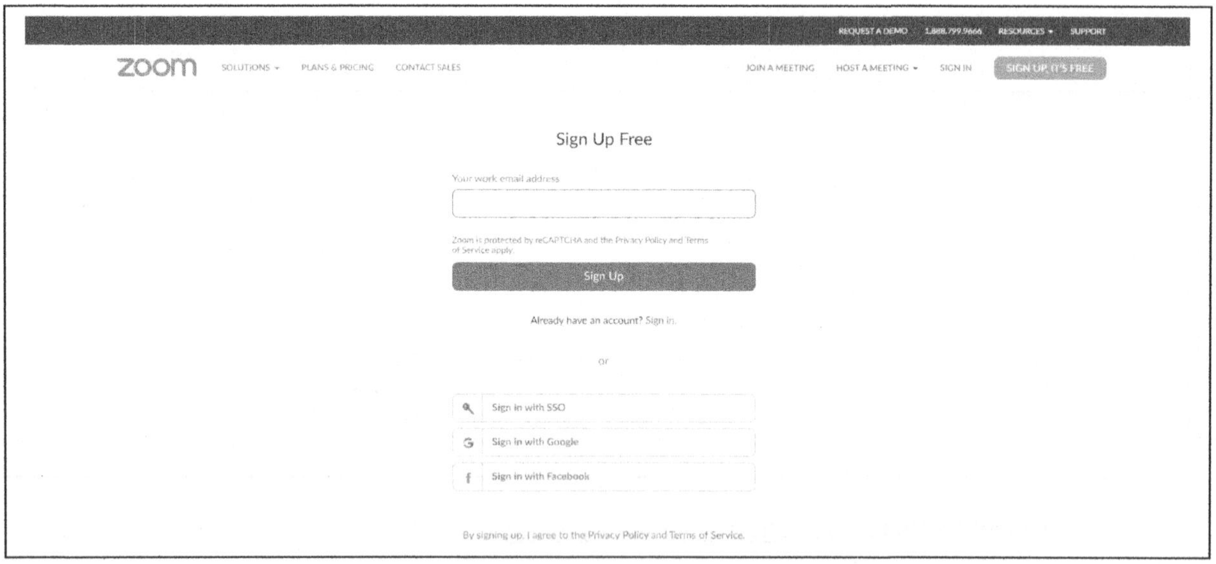

Figure 4 Zoom *Sign Up* or *Sign In* webpage.

5) Enter your email address. If you have previously made an account, left-click on *Sign In* in Figure 4 the Zoom user profile will appear. The user can then skip ahead to procedure step 14) after Figure 6.
6) If you did not left-click on *Sign In* then left-click on *Sign Up*. Figure 5 will appear on the screen and Zoom will send you a confirmation email.

Figure 5 Zoom email check webpage.

7) On the email left-click on *Activate Account*.
8) On the screen that appears answer: *Are you signing up on behalf of a school*? Then left-click on *Continue.*
9) *Welcome to Zoom* will appear.
10) Put in *First Name*, *Last Name* and a *Password.*
11) To keep things simpler do not invite colleagues to create their own Zoom accounts at this time. Select *Skip this step*.
12) *Your personal meeting URL* appears. It would look something like https://us04web.zoom.us/j/5881388953?pwd=cjP5R1JEU0F1enBJcTgxSVNZenRxQT09.
13) There is a choice to select either *Start Meeting Now* or *Go to My Account.* For simplicity, it is best to simply select *Go to My Account* now and do *Start Meeting* later. Figure 6 shows the result of steps 7) to 13).

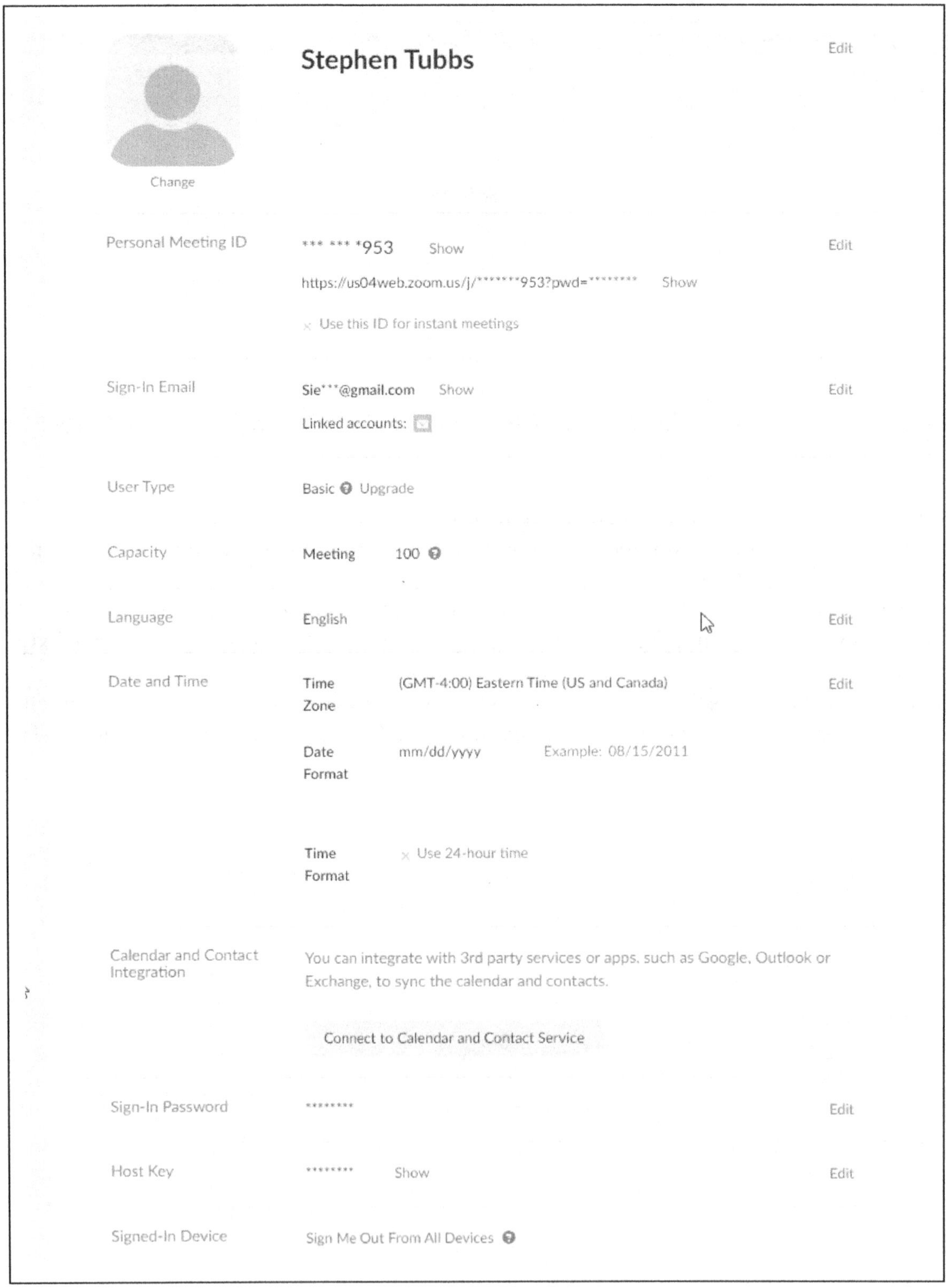

Figure 6 Zoom user profile.

14) The user should check that his *Time Zone* is correct and correct it if it is not.
15) The user should click *Show* on the *Personal Meeting ID, Sign-In Email and Host Key*. He should record all of those and his *Sign-In Password* in a safe place.

2.4.4 INSTALLING ZOOM BASIC WHILE JOINING A MEETING

Often the first a person learns about Zoom is through an invitation email to be a Zoom meeting participant. The invitation may look like Figure 7.

> Stephen Tubbs is inviting you to a scheduled Zoom meeting.
>
> Topic: Video conference 1
> Time: Aug 20, 2020 09:30 PM Eastern Time (US and Canada)
>
> Join Zoom Meeting
> https://us04,zoom,us/j/75902470959?pwd=V09bMmhZdVJaQTZUejhVbzhzNOpMZz09
>
> Meeting ID: 759 0247 0959

Figure 7 Typical invitation to a Zoom meeting.

When the email recipient goes to the invitation's website and he already has Zoom video conferencing software on his computer, Zoom will automatically launch and he will be able to join the meeting as a participant. If he does not yet have the Zoom software on his computer, he would automatically be directed to download Zoom in a procedure similar to that of Section 2.4.3. After installing Zoom, he will be able to attend the meeting as a participant.

2.4.5 ZOOM MEETING

There are two types of meetings, *Meet Now Meetings* and *Scheduled Meetings*. The host chooses one when setting up the meeting. Since the participant does not set up meetings, there is little difference for him.

2.4.5.1 ZOOM TEST MEETING

When first using Zoom (or first using it on an unfamiliar computer system) there can be surprises. Sometimes it just doesn't work. You can test your internet connection and the Zoom software without entering an actual meeting.

1) Go to a browser such as Google.
2) Go to https://zoom.us/test.
3) Left-click on *Join.*
4) Follow instructions to test the video camera, microphone and speaker.

2.4.5.2 JOINING A ZOOM MEETING AS A PARTICIPANT

A participant may learn about a Zoom meeting from an invitation like that in Figure 7.

The participant can select from options in Zoom. The host has even more options. Figure 8 shows the author as a participant who was the first at this Zoom meeting, even before the host.

Figure 8 The author as a participant logged into a Zoom meeting. The control options are described in Table 1 on the following page. Author note; Please forgive my oversized portrait I had to blow it up so the tiny control icons could be seen.

Control Icon	Screen Location	Main Purpose
 Mute microphone and pull down menu next to microphone.	Bottom left	Participant microphone on/off, Off indicated by a red slash and microphone & speaker selections and microphone and speaker test.
 Start/Stop video camera and pull down menu symbol next to the video camera	Bottom, 2nd from left	Participant camera on/off, Off indicated by a red slash and camera selection, virtual background, video settings.
 Participants	Bottom, 3rd from left	Total number of participants plus host. Left-clicking produces a list of Participants to right of screen.
 Chat	Bottom, 4th from left	Left-clicking this produces a list of participants and host on the right of the screen. By selecting participant and/or host names from the list one can chat with those people and not disturb others.
 Share Screen	Bottom, 5th from left	If the host has given permission, this allows the participant to put his screens from MS Word and other software on screen so they can be seen by others. It also allows the participant to markup screens using the cursor as a marking pen.
 Record	Bottom, 6th from left.	If the host permits it, the participant can record the meeting.

Continued

 Reactions	Bottom, 7th from left	Allows the participant to respond to something displayed on Zoom with a symbol of clapping hands or of thumb-up or thumb-down.
 Leave	Bottom right	Left-clicking on this will leave the meeting.
 Little circle	Top left	Zoom information about the meeting.
 Small shield	Top 2nd from left	This states that the meeting is encrypted and gives Zoom video conferencing software details.
 Screen size	Top right	Full or smaller screen display selector.

Table 1 Participant options.

2.4.5.3 STARTING A MEETING AS A HOST

There are *Meet Now Meetings (*also called *Instant Meetings)* and *Scheduled Meetings*. The *Meet Now Meeting* has little advance notice. The host setting it up might inform participants by email, text or phone to log into a certain Zoom web address right away or soon. A *Scheduled Meeting* has a time slot setup in advance. *Scheduled Meetings* can be one time meetings or repeating regularly run meetings. An example of a regularly *Scheduled Meeting* might be a school class that meets Tuesdays and Thursdays from 10 to 11 A.M. Once the meetings are underway *Meet Now Meetings* and *Scheduled Meetings* operate the same way.

2.4.5.3.1 STARTING A *MEET NOW* MEETING AS A HOST

1) If necessary load in Zoom using the procedure of Section 2.4.3.
2) Start Zoom. Figure 9 appears.

Figure 9 Zoom entry webpage.

3) Left-click on *Sign In*. Figure 10 appears.

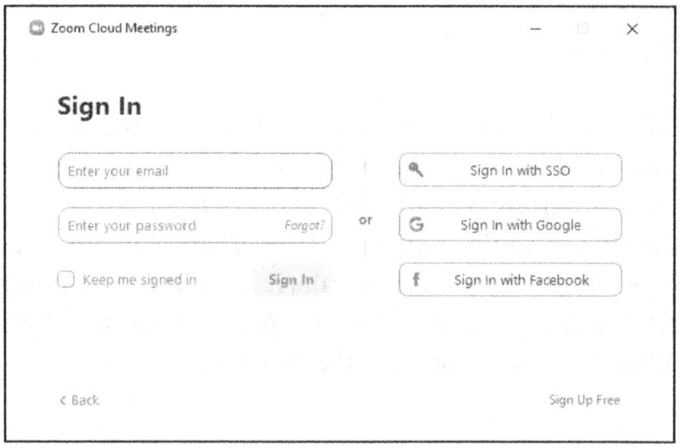

Figure 10 Zoom *Sign In* webpage.

4) *Enter your email*, *Enter your password* and left-click on *Sign In*. Figure 11 appears.

Figure 11 Zoom selection webpage.

5) Left-click on *New Meeting*. Figure 12 appears.

Figure 12 Host logged by himself into a Zoom meeting. The control options are described in Table 2 on the following page.

Control Icon	Screen Location	Main Purpose
 Mute microphone and pull down menu next to microphone.	Bottom left	Host microphone on/off, Off indicated by a red slash and microphone & speaker selections and microphone and speaker test.
 Start/Stop video camera and pull down menu symbol next to the video camera	Bottom, 2nd from left	Host camera on/off, Off indicated by a red slash and camera selection, virtual background, video settings.
 Security	Bottom, 3rd from left	Lock meeting and enable waiting room Allow/disallow participants to Share Screen, Chat, & Rename themselves.
 Participants	Bottom, 4th from left	Total number of participants plus host.
 Chat	Bottom, 5th from left	By selecting this and selecting participant and/or host names in a column list one can chat with those people and not disturb others.
 Share Screen and pull down menu next to Share Screen	Bottom, 6th from left	This allows the host to put his computer screens from MS Word and other software on screen so they can be seen by participants. It also allows the participant to markup screens using his cursor as a marking pen. On the pull down there are a number of Share Screen options. One important one is the host can permit or deny participants to Share Screen.

Continued

 Record	Bottom, 7th from left.	Allows host to record meeting, if desired.
 Reactions	Bottom, 8th from left	Allows the host to respond to something displayed on Zoom with a symbol of clapping hands or of thumb-up or thumb-down..
 End	Bottom right	Left-clicking on this will end the meeting for everyone.
 Little circle	Top left	Zoom information about the meeting.
 Small shield	Top 2nd from left	This states that the meeting is encrypted, gives Zoom video conferencing software details, and presents optional settings.
 Screen size	Top right	Full screen/smaller screen selector.

Table 2 Host options.

6) On the bottom of the screen left-click on *Participants*. Figure 13 appears.

Figure 13 Host logged by himself into a Zoom meeting. The white section on the right shows participants. More will be listed during the meeting as more participants join.

7) At the bottom of the white section on the right left-click on *Invite*. Figure 14 appears.

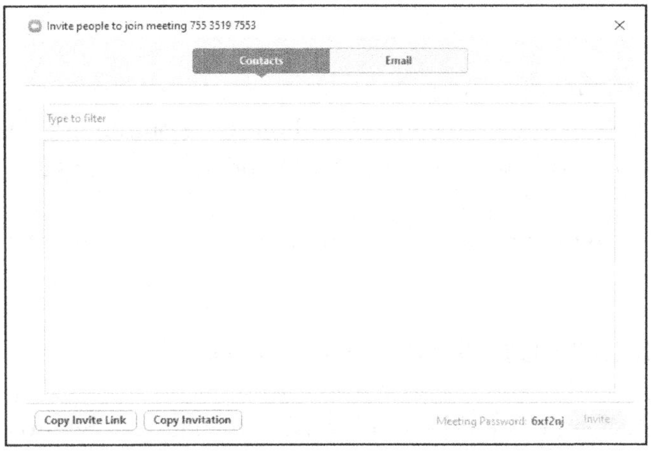

Figure 14 List of people invited to meeting.

8) Left-click on Email to enter email addresses to be notified of the meeting. Figure 15 appears.

Figure 15 Choosing email service to send invitations.

9) Gmail works well with Zoom. If you have a Gmail account, select it. Figure 16 appears.

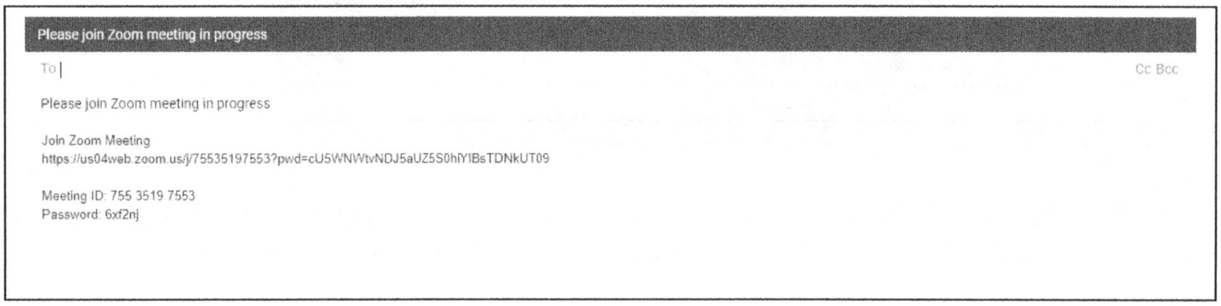

Figure 16 Meeting notice web page. Note this web page is taller than shown here. At the bottom left of it is the *Send* command.

10) Put the list of emails into Figure 16 after *To*.
11) At the bottom of the meeting notice web page of Figure 16 on the left, left-click on *Send* to send notices to the email addresses. (Note: *Send* is not shown in Figure 16 but will appear on your screen.)
12) When the participant(s) go to the address shown in the email message the meeting begins.

2.4.5.3.2 STARTING A SCHEDULED MEETING AS A HOST

1) If Zoom has not already been installed, install it using the steps in Section 2.4.3.
2) Start Zoom. The web page will be as seen in Figure 9.
3) *Sign In* with Zoom. As in Figure 10.
4) *Enter your email*, *Enter your password* and left-click on *Sign In*. Figure 11 appears.
5) Select *Schedule*. A webpage will appear that allows you to enter details on the meeting(s) you wish to schedule. See Figure 17.

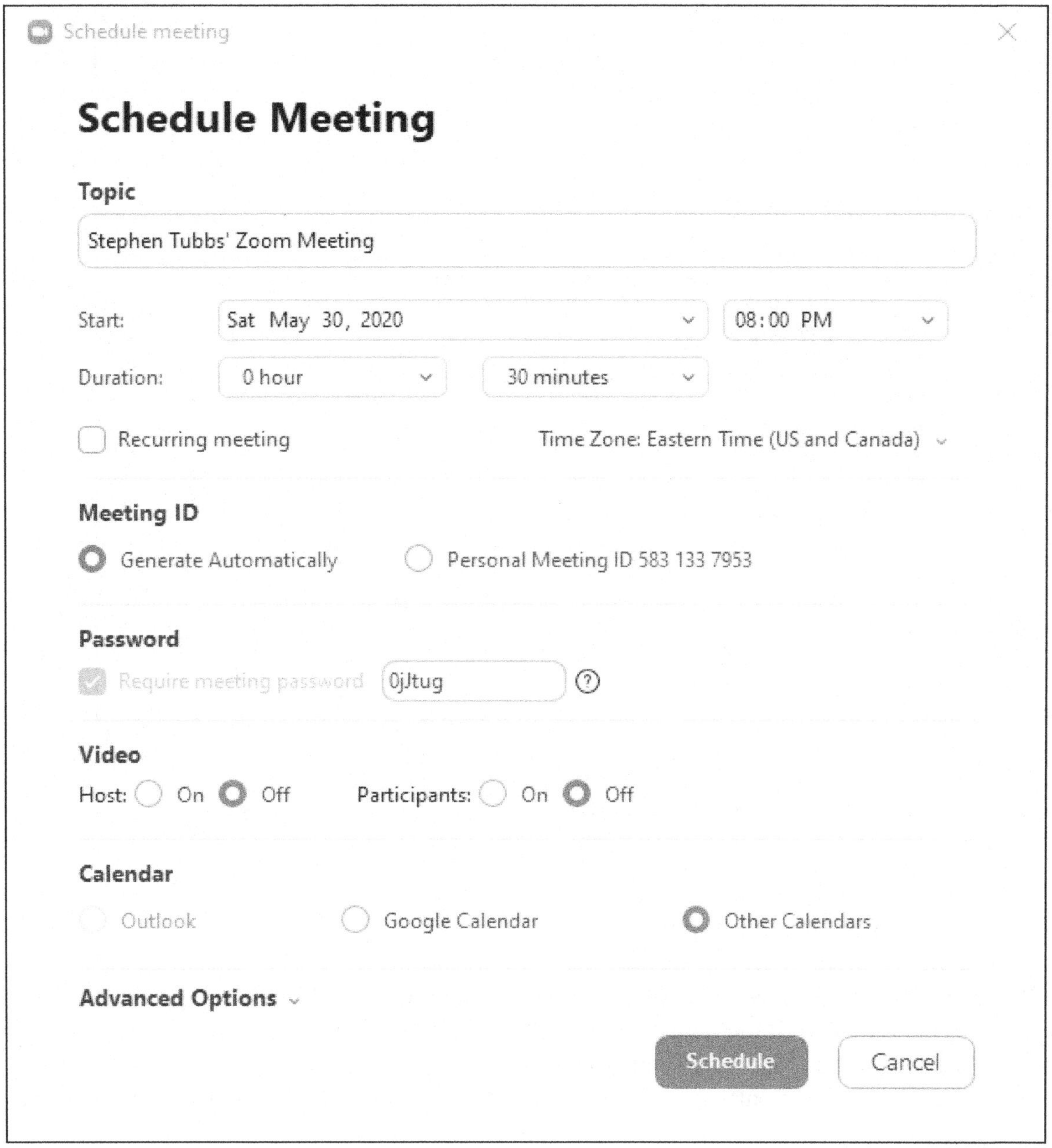

Figure 17 Schedule Meeting webpage.

6) Left-click on *Schedule*.
7) Figure 18 appears. It calls for a single meeting that will be set up similarly to a *Now Meeting*, however it will be at a specific future time. (in the example case: May 30, 2020 at 8:00 pm for 30 minutes).

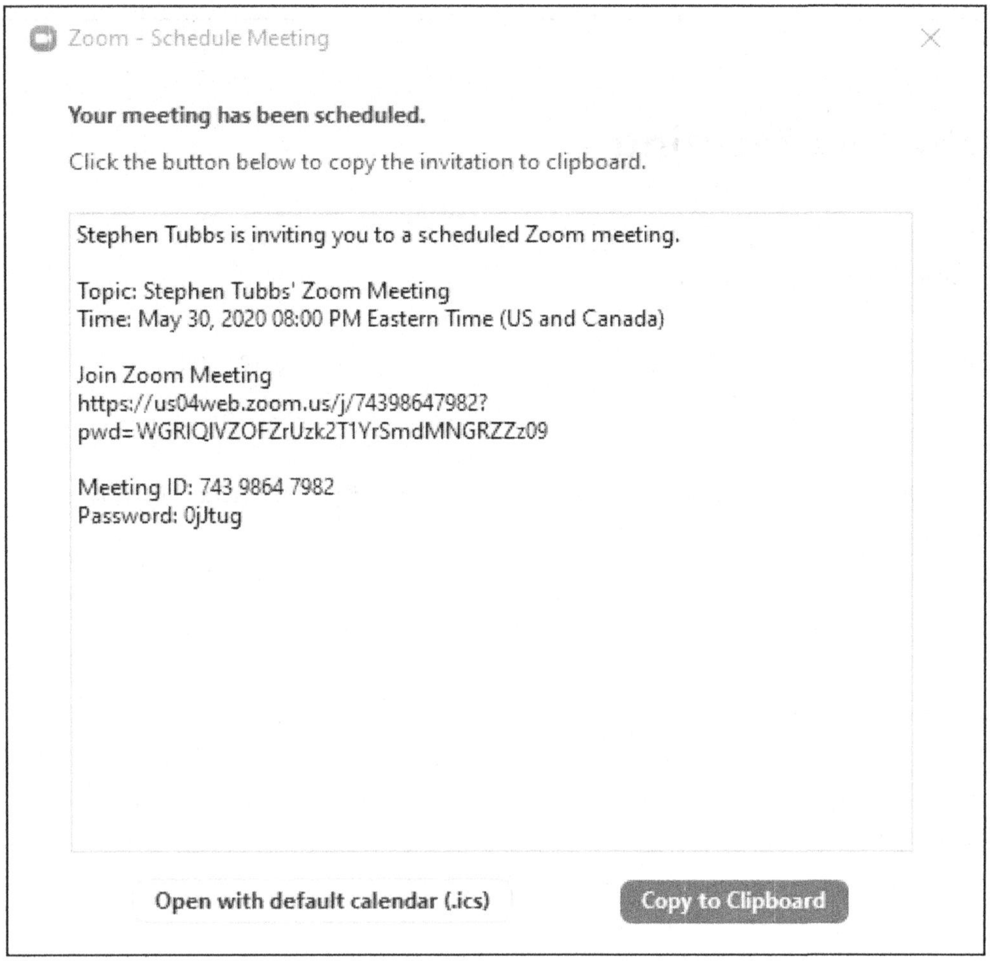

Figure 18 One time meeting invitation.

8) Left-click on *Copy to Clipboard*. As an alternative to using Clipboard, you can simply highlight the text of the notice and use Ctrl C to copy the notice and Ctrl V to paste it into a notice email that you would send to participants.
9) When the host and participants signs into the meeting shortly before the start time, this start the meeting.
10) Alternatively, if in step 6) a recurring meeting had been selected in Figure 17 the web page of Figure 19 would have appeared.

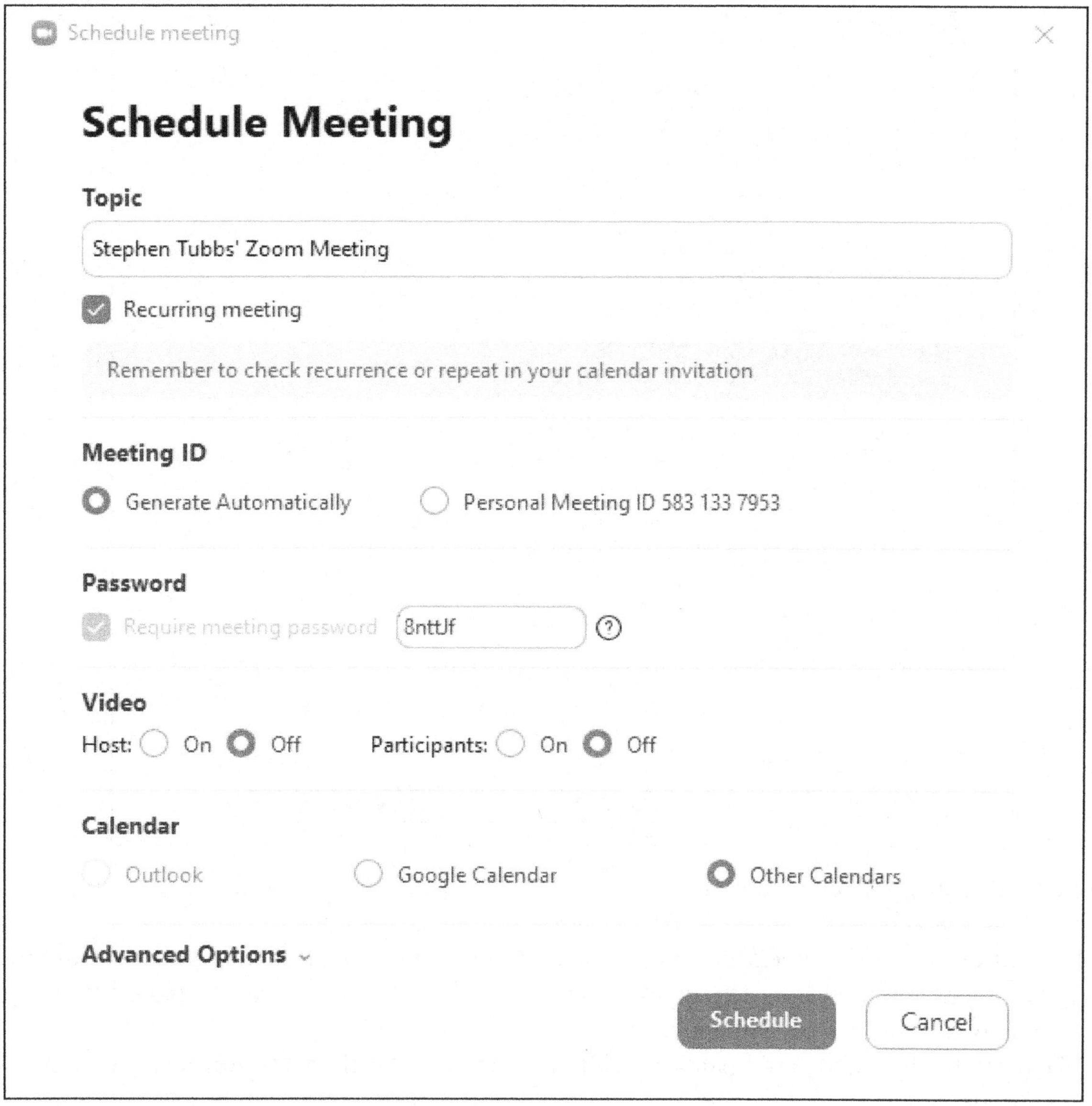

Figure 19 When a recurring meeting is selected.

11) Make other selections as desired and then left-click on *Schedule*.
12) Figure 20 appears.

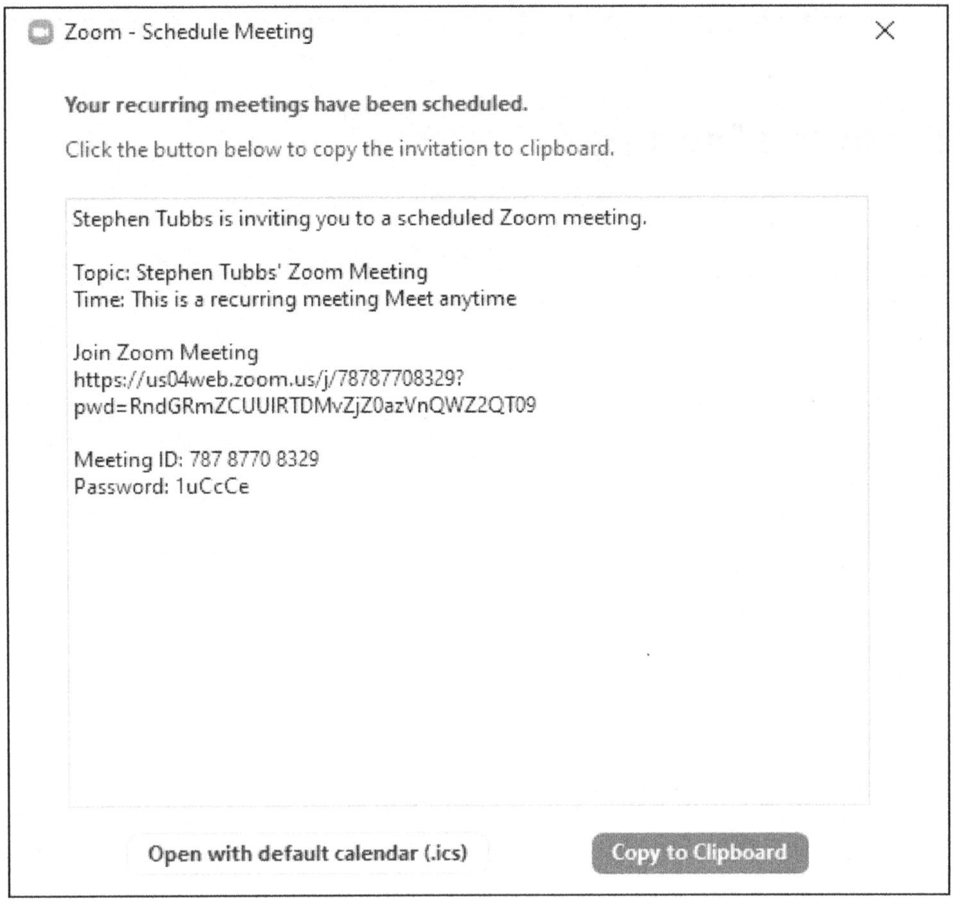

Figure 20 Recurring meeting invitation.

13) Left-click on *Copy to Clipboard*. As an alternative to using Clipboard, you can simply highlight and use Ctrl C to copy the notice and Ctrl V to paste it into a notice email that you would send to participants.
14) When the host and participants sign into the meeting shortly before the start time, this start the meeting.

2.4.5.4 SOME IMPORTANT ZOOM FEATURES

Zoom has many useful controls and features. Some of the most useful are described below.

2.4.5.4.1 MUTE

The *Mute* command on the bottom left of a participant's and host's screen will turn off their microphone when left-clicked. On the screen a microphone with a red slash across it is turned off.

In all but the smallest meetings it is best to reduce background noise. Unused microphones should be muted.

The host also has *Mute All* selector on the right side of his screen under the participant's list. This would be best used in large meetings where participant feedback is less important than reducing background noise.

When muted, the participants can still make comments via text using the Chat icon.

2.4.5.4.2 START/STOP VIDEO

Next to the *Mute* command is the *Start/Stop* video command. It is on both the host's and participant's controls.

A host's or participant's camera is off when a red slash appears across his camera icon. When it is off others cannot see him. It is good for a bad hair day.

2.4.5.4.3 CHAT

The *Chat* command is also on the bottom of the host and participants' screens. *Chat* allows a host and participants to speak in small groups via text without disturbing the main meeting.

2.4.5.4.4 SHARE SCREEN

This very useful feature allows the host and the participants (with the host's permission) to display screens that are on their own computers.

For example, if the host has a MS Word document that he would like to show the meeting participants, he would start MS Word while the meeting is in progress and open the document. Then he would go to Zoom and select *Share Screen*. The MS Word document would appear on the host's computer screen in miniature. When the host selects that MS Word document miniature the host will then see it in full size on his computer screen and the participants will also see it on their computer screens. When doing MS Word documents the document can be interacted with, just as if it can when being word processed.

More information can be gotten from the Share Your Screen selection in https://zoom.us/resources.

2.4.5.4.5 RECORD A MEETING

A host and/or a participant with the host's permission can record a meeting. Both Host and participants have *Record* icons.

There a number of online videos on how to record a meeting. One of those can be found on https://zoom.us/resources.

2.5 ZOOM ON AN IPHONE

It is possible to use many Zoom PC features on an iPhone or iPad. The ruggedness and portability of the iPhone and iPad can make them very useful in some circumstances. However, the small screens and more awkward keyboards can make them more difficult to use if screen detail or much typing is needed.

The instructions below apply to an iPhone. They were written for use on an iPhone 6s.

2.5.1 INSTALLING ZOOM

1) Go to your iPhone's *APP Store*.
2) Search for and select the *Zoom APP*,
3) Open *ZOOM Cloud Meetings*. Figure 21 will appear.

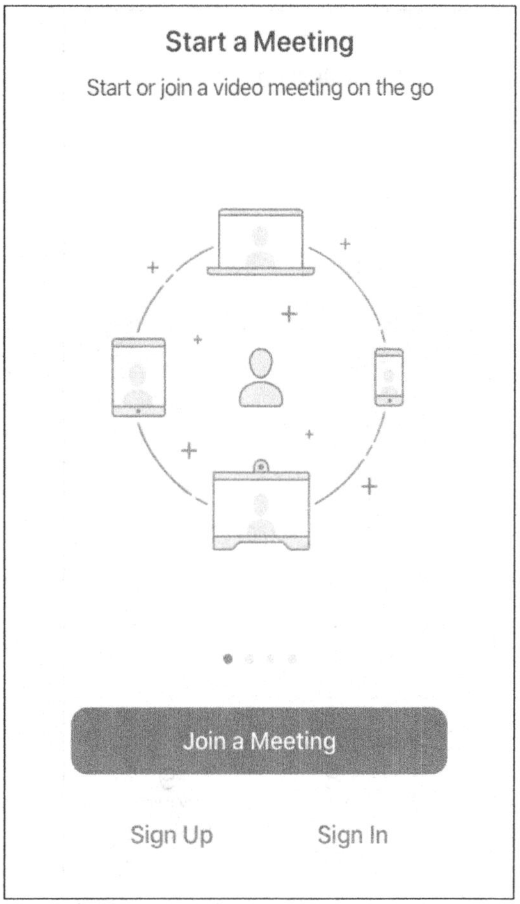

Figure 21 iPhone screen after first loading in Zoom.

4) Choose *Sign Up*.
5) Put in your date of birth.
6) Put in your *Email Address*, *First Name*, *Last Name* and agree to the *Terms of Service*. Then select *Sign Up*.
7) A confirmation email message will be sent to the email address. Click the confirmation link to start your iPhone's Zoom account.

2.5.2 BEING A PARTICIPANT

1) Start Zoom. Figure 21 appears.
2) Select *Join a Meeting*. Figure 22 appears.

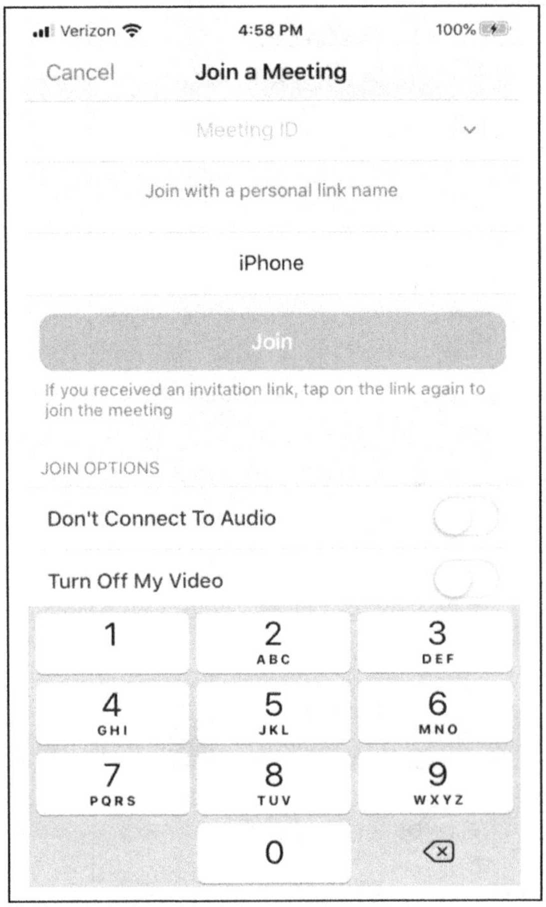

Figure 22 iPhone screen to *Join a Meeting*.

3) Enter the desired *Meeting ID* and touch *Join*.
4) A screen will appear that asks for your *Password*.
5) A *Video Preview* screen appears. See Figure 23.

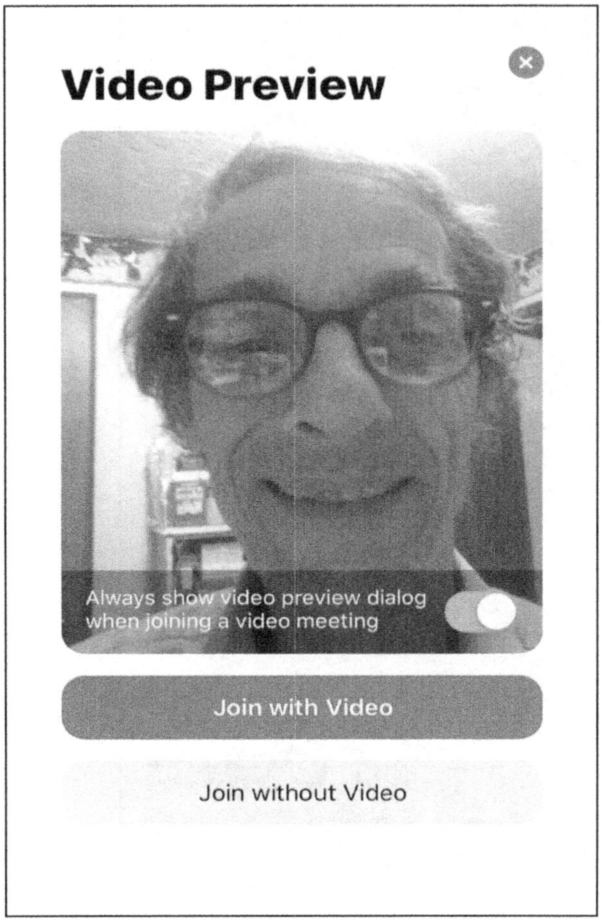

Figure 23 Preview.

6) Touch *Join with Video*. Figure 24 appears.

Figure 24 Participant's iPhone screen. Notice how similar it is to that of Figure 8 where the author, as a participant, was logged into a Zoom meeting with a PC.

2.5.3 BEING A HOST

1) Start Zoom. Figure 21 appears.
2) Select *Sign In*. Figure 25 appears.

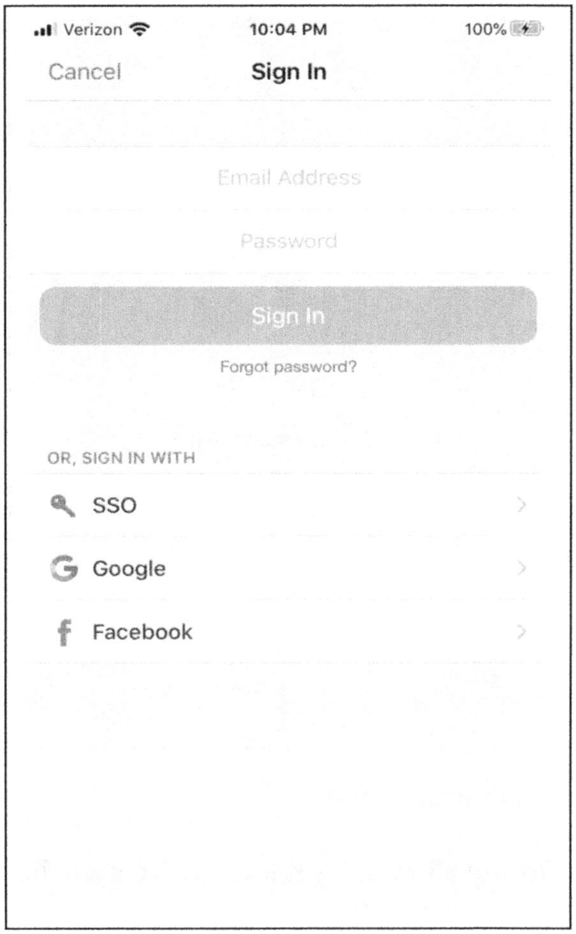

Figure 25 iPhone screen to *Sign In* to a meeting.

3) Enter your *Email Address* and *Password*
4) Zoom will ask to access your calendar. Select *Don't Allow* to keep things simpler.
5) Zoom will ask if *you would like to use Siri with Zoom?* Answer *No* to keep things simpler.
6) Zoom will ask if you would like to sign in with *Touch ID*? Answer *No* to keep things simpler.
7) Zoom now gives you a number of options. See Figure 26.

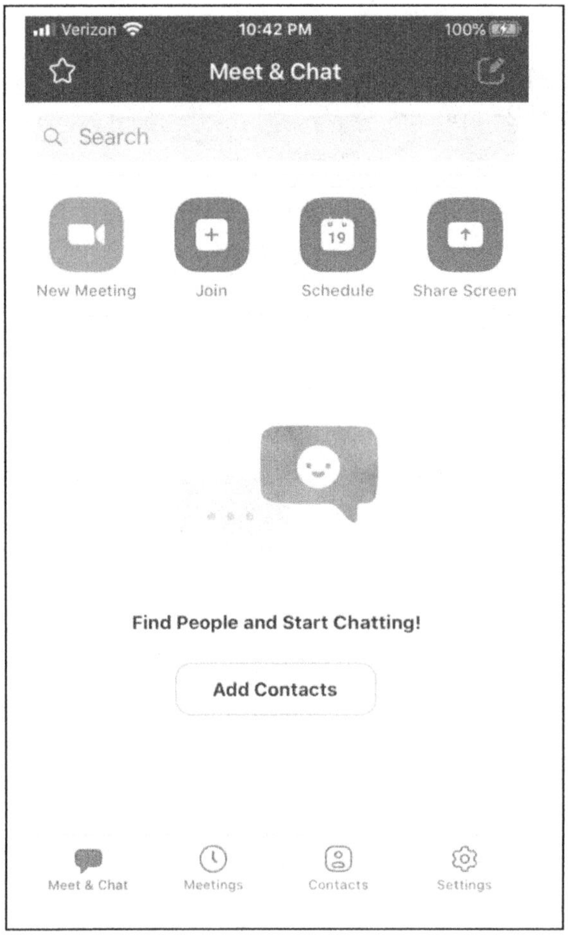

Figure 26 iPhone screen to select meeting to host.

8) The screen in Figure 26 will allow many selections. To keep things simpler here touch *New Meeting*. The screen of Figure 27 appears.

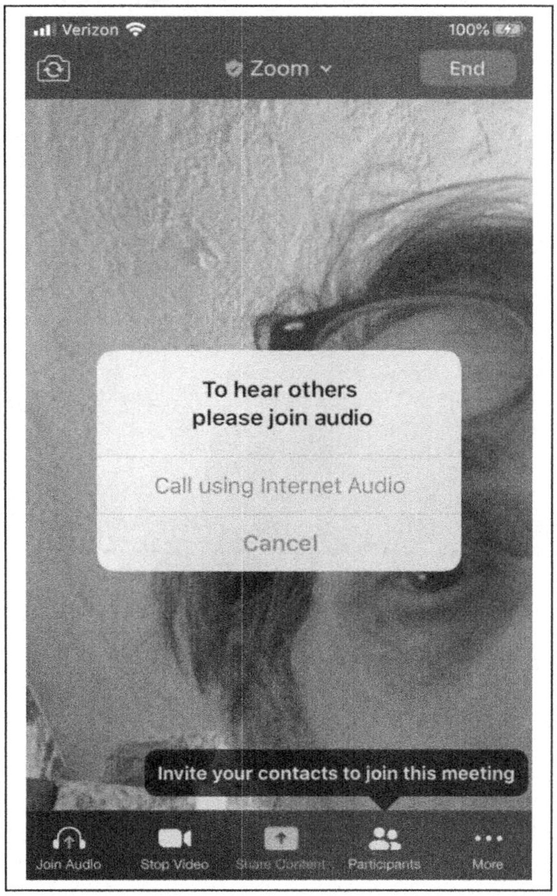

Figure 27 iPhone *New Meeting* screen.

9) Select *Call using internet Audio*.
10) Touch the Participants icon and Figure 28 appears.

Figure 28 iPhone *Participants Invitation* list, *Invite* command and *Mute All* command.

11) As with the PC in Figure 13 participants invited with the *Invite* command of Figure 28.
12) An example of an emailed invitation is in Figure 29.

Join Zoom Meeting

http://us04web.zoom.us/j/7107165268?
pwd=ejFwWVdZWXd4Y2YyTytONTIvUm8wQT09

Meeting ID: 710 1716 5268
Password: 3tSXCQ

Sent from my iPhone

Figure 29 Typical email invitation to a one time Zoom Meeting as sent from an iPhone.

2.6 ZOOM ON A MAC

Zoom has instructions on how to install it on a Mac. See https://support.zoom.us/hc/en-us/articles/203020795-How-To-Install-on-Mac.

Once the Zoom video conferencing software is installed and operating it should function very much like it does on a PC as described in Section 2.4.

3.0 MISCELLANEOUS

3.1 ZOOM AUDIO CONFERENCING

Zoom Audio Conferencing can be most easily thought of as Zoom Video Conferencing without the video. It allows a person to join or host a Zoom Video Conference through a telephone without a screen.

Zoom Audio Conferencing can be phone-only meetings.

Zoom Audio Conferencing is not free. There may be a dial-in charge and there are phone per minute charges in many countries.

For more details see https://support.zoom.us/hc/en-us/articles/201362663-Join-by-Telephone#h_682f2e00-6a7c-4a5a-b20f-70b9b9012563 and https://support.zoom.us/hc/en-us/articles/201362663-Join-by-Telephone.

3.2 ZOOM VIDEO WEBINARS

A webinar is a live online presentation that allows viewers to ask questions and give comments to the presenter.

A Zoom Video Webinar is similar to a Zoom Meeting in many ways. However a Zoom Video Webinar can handle many more viewers, up to 10,000. Also, a Zoom Webinar viewer has fewer feedback options than a Zoom Meeting participant.

Information on Zoom Webinars is on https://zoom.us/webinar.

3.3 ZOOM FOR GOVERNMENT

Zoom for government is a special version of Zoom made and controlled by U.S. citizens for use by the U.S. government agencies and their contractors. Its abbreviated name is Zoomgov.

Zoomgov has all the same features that are found within the commercial versions of Zoom (the versions the main subject of this book.). However, Zoomgov operates in a dedicated, secure infrastructure designed to meet the requirements of FedRAMP (Federal Risk and Authorization Management Program) Moderate baseline and DOD (Department of Defense) Impact Level 2.

More information on Zoom for Government is available on https://www.zoomgov.com/.

3.4 ZOOM SECURITY FLAWS AND CONCERNS

Zoom has had problems with privacy and security. One of the problems was and may still be with "Zoom-bombings" where a hacker enters a chat room to put in uncalled for language. Another problem was a bug in the Zoom video conferencing software that allowed a hacker to take over a Zoom user's Mac.

Should users avoid Zoom? If they are discussing important state or industrial secrets avoiding Zoom would probably be reasonable. However, for non-secret matters that most of us deal with it is probably good enough. For example, students discussing homework assignments don't have too much too worry about.

One practical precaution a host can implement in Zoom meetings is to ask participants to sign in with a password.

Zoom has information on security on https://zoom.us/security.

3.5 POPULAR VIDEO CONFERENCING SOFTWARE

There are many video conferencing software available. In May 2020 PCMag.com listed what it considered to be the ten best on https://www.pcmag.com/picks/the-best-video-conferencing-software. Each of these software should be used with a computer or smartphone that has a webcam, microphone, and speaker or earphones.

The ten PCMag.com software were searched for as job requirements on a popular job website. From that search the three most requested software of the PCMag.com list are listed below.

1) Microsoft Teams

   Primary audience: business users of Microsoft 365
   Headquarters location: Redmond, Washington
   When first developed: March 2017
   Website: https://www.microsoft.com/en-us/microsoft-365/microsoft-teams/group-chat-software
   Largest meetings allowed: 10,000 in a team
   Costs[1]: Free to $20.00/user/month
   Computer systems it will operate on: Windows Server 2012 R2+, Windows 10 or Windows 8.1 in 32-bit and 64-bit. For the best experience, use the latest version of your operating system. Mac OS X 10.11 El Capitan or later. Linux distribution capable of installing DEB or RPM.
   Number of mentions in job descriptions in the popular job website in July 2020: 2131
   Author's opinion: Microsoft Teams is especially meant to go with Microsoft Office-365.

2) Zoom

   Primary audience: Everybody, business and social
   Headquarters location; San Jose, California
   When first developed: Zoom software available 2013
   Website: https://zoom.us/
   Largest meetings allowed: 1000 participants, 10,000 webinar attendees
   Costs[1]: Free to $19.99/month/host
   Computer systems it will operate on: See details in Section 2.2.
   Number of mentions in job descriptions in the popular job website in July 2020: 1785

3) Cisco WebEx
    Primary audience: Business
    Headquarters location: Milpitas, California
    When first developed: WebEx company began in 1995, in 1999 they released meetings software
    Website: https://www.webex.com/
    Largest meetings allowed: 200 participants, 3000 webinar attendees
    Costs[1]: Free to $26.95/month/host
    Computer systems it will operate on: Windows 7 32-bit/64-bit, 8 32-bit/64-bit, 8.1 32-bit/64-bit, Server 2008 64-bit, Server 2008 R2 64-bit, 10, 10 Enterprise LTSB; Mac OS X 10.13, 10.14, 10.15; Linux (Web App) (32-bit/64-bit) Ubuntu 14.x or later, OpenSuSE 13.x or later, Fedora 18 or later, Red Hat 6 or later, Debian 8.x or later
    Number of mentions in job descriptions in the popular job website in July 2020: 1264

So far, Facebook has not been considered to be video conferencing software. However, now Facebook has announced a new service, Facebook Messenger Rooms. Facebook Messenger Rooms allows meetings of up to 50 participants. 50 participant meetings are small compared to usual video conferencing software's capabilities. But, given the size and successes of Facebook, Inc. Facebook Messenger Rooms may soon be an important video conferencing software.

[1] Note: These costs are for use of the programs in interactive video conferencing. The program costs can be higher for large webinars and some other uses of the programs.

3.6 ZOOM GLOSSARY AND MISCELLANEOUS INFORMATION

The following words and word combinations appear in Zoom literature. It is hoped the short definitions and descriptions provided will make it easier to understand Zoom and its literature. Note the definitions given here are not general definitions, they are written for Zoom and similar systems.

AES 256-bit Encryption: A trusted computer data encryption method.

App: Is a modern term for application software. This software is designed do a specific function for the user. The term app is more common on mobile devices but may also be used with desktop computers..

Attendee: For Zoom an attendee listens and participated in a Zoom meeting, but does not control it. The host controls it. For example, an attendee may speak in a Zoom meeting, but only if allowed to do so by the host.

Audio Feedback: If the microphone is too close to the speaker sound will be picked up by the microphone amplified and played back louder by the speaker. An earphone/microphone headset is recommended by Zoom to reduce audio feedback.

Background Noise: Extraneous noise that a sound system makes.

Calendar, Google and Yahoo: Free calendar apps from Google and Yahoo that can be used with Zoom.

Carrier: Phone company. Some examples would be Verizon and AT&T.

Chat: In video conferencing this is a method of sending text messages to other attendees or the host without sending them to all those in the meeting. In Zoom the host has the option to stop chat messages. See section 2.4.5.4.3

Cloud Computing: Storing and receiving data and programs over the internet rather than a local hard drive.

Co host[2]: The host can share meeting or webinar hosting privileges with another user, allowing the co-host to manage the administrative side of the meeting, such as managing participants or starting/stopping the recording. Only the host can assign a co-host.

Cookies: Small files from a visited website's webserver that are stored on a user's hard drive.

Download: Copy from one computer system to another, typically over the Internet.

GCM Encryption[2]: Stands for Galois/Counter Mode Encryption.

Gmail: A free email service developed by Google LLC.

IO Device: Is an Input/output device, any hardware used by a human operator or other systems to communicate with a computer.

Mobile App: Also called a mobile application or simply an app, is a computer program or software application designed to run on a mobile device such as a phone, tablet or watch.

Mute: See section 2.4.5.4.1

Outlook.com: It is a free, personal email service from Microsoft.

Record a Meeting: See section 2.4.5.4.5.

Share Screen: See section 2.4.5.4.4

Start/Stop Video: See section 2.4.5.4.2

URL: Short for Uniform Resource Locator. It is a web address.

USB: Universal serial bus, a standardized technology for attaching peripheral devices to a computer.

Video Conferencing: The holding of a conference among people at remote locations by means of transmitted audio and video signals.

VoIP[2]: Voice over Internet Protocol. This applies to Zoom Phone.

Zoom Chat[2] (see https://zoom.us/feature/messaging) This is more than the Chat that appears on participants' and host's screens. Zoom Chat is a way of organizing teams of workers to better streamline communication, collaboration and creativity of teams.

Zoom Host: In a Zoom meeting the host controls various aspects of the meeting. He is in charge of the meeting and is usually the presenter.

Zoom *Meet Now Meeting* (Instant Meeting): This is the alternative to the Zoom Scheduled Meeting. A *Meet Now Meeting* starts instantly and you can invite others to join the meeting at any time. You can use your *Personal Meeting ID* for *Meet Now Meeting*s.

Zoom *Meeting*: An online event where one person hosts and all other participants have equal footing. The host can share hosting responsibilities with other participants. Any participant can share their screen provided the host allows it..

Zoom Music mode[2]: Zoom is optimized for human speech and the associated frequency range and volume levels. There are settings you can change to optimize Zoom for the dynamic range of music.

Zoom Participant: A Zoom participant is an invitee in a meeting scheduled by a Zoom Host. A participant does not require a Zoom account in order to join a meeting. Participants can join a meeting from their phone, desktop, mobile and tablet devices.

Zoom Personal Audio Conference[2]: High definition telephone conferencing system similar to a traditional phone conferencing system, but through Zoom and a computer system.

Zoom *Personal Meeting ID*: ID for a Personal Meeting Room.

Zoom Personal Meeting Room: Your Personal Meeting Room is a virtual meeting room permanently reserved for you that you can access with your Personal Meeting ID (PMI). Your Personal Meeting Room is good for meeting with people that you meet with regularly.

Zoom Phone[2] A modern cloud phone system add-on to an existing Zoom subscription. It makes phone calls without the video.

Zoom Polling: A host is able to provide questions that the participants can vote on.

Zoom Rooms[2]: Zoom rents virtual video conference rooms that can be used by groups of people. Zoom rooms allows one physical room of people to interact with people that may be far away in other locations. Information on Zoom Rooms is on https://zoom.us/zoomrooms.

Zoom Scheduled Meeting: See section 2.4.5.3.2

Zoom Security Flaws: See section 3.4

Zoom Video Webinar[2]: See section 3.2

Zoom Virtual Background: The Virtual Background feature allows you to display an image or video as your background during a Zoom Meeting.

Zoom Web Client: Allows joining a Zoom meeting or webinar without downloading any plugins or software.

[2]This term applies to uses of Zoom that are more advanced than needed for creating and attending BASIC online Zoom meetings.

Made in the USA
Monee, IL
08 November 2026

67378683R00031